EIGHT
HONG KONG
POETS

A Chameleon Press book

EIGHT HONG KONG POETS
ISBN 978-988-13642-6-5

© 2015 the individual poets
and Chameleon Press

Published by Chameleon Press Ltd.
15/F, 1506-7 Pacific Plaza, 418 Des Voeux Road West, Hong Kong
www.chameleonpress.com

First printing 2015

Credits and acknowledgements
Except as noted below, poems first appear in collections published by Chameleon Press.
—
Tim Kaiser's "Statues" first appeared in the literary journal *Cha*.
—
Leung Ping-kwan's poems are reproduced by permission of the the Leung Ping-kwan estate.
—
Shirley Geok-Lin Lim's poems appear in *Do You Live In?* (Ethos Books).
—
Sarah Howe's poems appear in *Loop of Jade* (Chatto & Windus).
They are reproduced by permission of The Random House Group Ltd.

All rights reserved. No part of this book may be reproduced in any form or by any electronic means, including information storage and retrieval systems, without permission in writing from the publisher, except by a reviewer who may quote brief passages in a review. The right of the contributing poets to be identified as the Authors of the Work has been asserted as have their moral rights with respect to the Work.

EIGHT HONG KONG POETS

edited by
David McKirdy
Peter Gordon

Leung Ping-Kwan · Jennifer Wong
Shirley Geok-lin Lim · David McKirdy ·
Tammy Ho Lai-ming · Eddie Tay
Tim Kaiser · Sarah Howe

chameleon press
hong kong

*The editors dedicate this volume to
the memory of Leung Ping-kwan (1949-2013)*

PREFACE

IF OUR ENVIRONMENT shapes us as people, then the place in which we live must also inform our creative endeavours and shape us as poets. This has certainly been the case with my own writing. Hong Kong is frequently viewed and portrayed as the archetypal modern Asian city, with its thrusting architectural vernacular which is the main fodder of the documentary, travelogue and infomercial. Like something taken from Italo Calvino's book *Invisible Cities*, Hong Kong is a different place to different demographic groups and even to different individuals within these same groups.

My Hong Kong is the city of history, mythology and magic and I write these words from the summit of Flying Goose Mountain, one of the nine dragons from which Kowloon District derives its name. Mine is a city of bird-song, cicadas and bamboo windchimes, abandoned hamlets high on mountain passes and a story under every stone. In the midst of the metropolis we find hidden shrines shrouded in incense, fortune-tellers, apothecaries and acupuncturists as well as ancient crones under freeway flyovers who will for a small fee beat paper effigies of your enemies with a wooden shoe.

The name Hong Kong, or *Heung Gong* in the local Cantonese, means "Fragrant Harbour", but this does not, as many people believe, refer to the sweet smell of the sea air, for Hong Kong has in actuality always smelled of preserved fish and shrimp paste which hang in the same oppressive, humid air that pervades many Far Eastern trading ports.

For the last 100 years or more, it has also smelled of burnt coal and diesel from the countless ships and small vessels traversing the harbour, as well as the pungent aroma of raw sewage discharged at various points into the sea. New arrivals to Hong Kong would be assailed by the smell at the now closed Kai Tak Airport in the heart of the city and upon asking through handkerchiefs and gritted teeth what the smell was would be informed by "old hands": "that, my dear fellow, is the smell of money!"

Hong Kong's name is actually derived from its historical trade in incense and the "fragrant" in the name refers to the agar wood and sandalwood trees which were harvested to supply incense and joss sticks throughout China for devotional purposes. Several hundred years ago the trade was wiped out overnight by an edict from the emperor to clear all of the land within 25 miles of the sea to deprive a dissident pirate warlord of any food and support because of his opposition to the emperor. The trees were all cut down and the people dispersed only to return after a 50-year absence.

The history and legends of these people still dot the landscape by way of place names like "Yau Ma Tei"—Oil and Millet Fields, now concrete high-rise; "Sham Shui Po"—Deep Water Pier, miles from the sea; "Hung Hom"—Red Cliff, as flat as a plain; and "Yau Yat Chuen"—One More Village, a bucolic poetic concept amidst a dense city-scape.

Taken from a well-loved poem by the Sung Dynasty poet Lu Yu, here is the final stanza in translation:

Where the hills and streams end
there seems no road beyond
amidst the shady willows
and bright flowers
one more village.

TIME TRAVELS FASTER in Hong Kong than anywhere else and an absence of a few months can result in a return to a physical landscape where mirrored glass edifices full of designer retail outlets have replaced the run-down industrial units with tea shops, barbers and hardware stores that previously occupied the space. The access road may now be a four-lane highway a few metres from the original entrance.

This has always been a feature of life in Hong Kong and the years have seen the disappearance of many streets and buildings.

PREFACE

Even more poignant is the fading away of the human scenery that included, for better or worse, street scribes, rickshaw pullers, women with bound feet, knife sharpeners and itinerant herbalists—snake oil salesmen with live monkeys on a chain.

These images of a past, felt if not always remembered, feature in the work of many Hong Kong poets, including that of my fellow poets included in this anthology. Much of my own work has been an attempt to preserve some of these images for posterity.

The linguistic landscape is another source of poetic inspiration, with mispronunciations, mistranslations and misappropriations all adding richness to the emulsion. Contributions from Cantonese, English, Mandarin, Portuguese, Russian, Hindi, Nepali and Tagalog all add something to the mix, with place names, food and physical artefacts often transliterated into words that mean nothing in any of these languages but which are firmly incorporated into that unique mix of Hong Kong vernacular known as *yuen yeung*, named after the popular distinctive local drink consisting of half tea and half coffee. *Yuen yeung* literally means mandarin duck and is a reference to the fact that the male and female look completely different, this has thus become synonymous with two different but complimentary things—Hong Kong in a nutshell.

Although Hong Kong is 98 percent Chinese, it is a city of immigrants and has through world wars, revolutions and colonial diasporas, welcomed people from all parts of China and all over the world. Few people, families or communities are entrenched for more than a generation or two and many maintain cultural, linguistic, clan and culinary affinities related to their historic origins.

In such a mix, poets find a home that inspires and provokes in equal measure. I personally feel blessed to be able to observe my adopted city with an insider's knowledge, yet with the outsider's eye, and to call it home.

David McKirdy

COMPILING AN ANTHOLOGY of Hong Kong poetry presumes that there is such a thing. If there is, what is it? Properly posed, this is of course a two-part question, for Hong Kong writing in Chinese and English operate, like much of Hong Kong society, in largely separate spheres.

English, for its part, is the imposed colonial language which—despite sometimes committed and sometimes desultory efforts by government, educational institutions and the media to embed it more deeply—floats like a sheen of oil on the deeper pool that is Chinese.

And like oil, Hong Kong English and its practioners can evanesce only to be redeposited in other parts. Hong Kong poetry in English has been—at least since Chameleon Press published its first volume a dozen years ago—very much a story of poets who go, come, return and sometimes are in several places at once.

Yet in all this moving about, something of Hong Kong always remains.

We start this volume, as arguably all anthologies of Hong Kong poetry must, with the late Leung Ping-kwan, one of the very few Hong Kong poets or, indeed, writers of any kind, that managed to bridge the linguistic divide between Chinese and English. Originally written in Chinese, his work has been extensively translated, some by his own hand, more often in such tight cooperation with others that it now forms as much a part of the English-language corpus as the Chinese.

"Something sets us looking for a place," starts one of Sarah Howe's poems. People tend to end up in Hong Kong like that; I did. Eddie Tay, David McKirdy and Timothy Kaiser all came—from Singapore, Scotland and Canada, respectively—and never left, or at least haven't yet.

Sarah Howe, Jennifer Wong and Tammy Ho Lai-ming, conversely, were born here. Howe and Wong now reside in Britain,

PREFACE

Howe having left while a child, Wong for university. Ho attended graduate school in London, but now teaches in Hong Kong.

Some, much like the ships which figure in more than one poem here, come and stay for a while, go and return. Shirley Geok-lin Lim is originally from Malacca, now teaches in the United States and has several stints teaching in Hong Kong, the latest coinciding with the recent "umbrella movement"; the poems included here, which come from her upcoming collection, date from this period.

This, then, is Hong Kong poetry: that something that is left when all other influences are peeled away. People who know Hong Kong will recognise it instantly.

The poems in this collection are, with only one or two exceptions, taken from published collections. If you like the poets sampled here, we hope you will seek out their complete volumes.

Peter Gordon

Contents

1	**Leung Ping-kwan**
2	Central
3	Wanchai
4	Ladder Street
5	An Old Colonial Building
6	Kuafu at Exchange Square
8	Postcards of Old Hong Kong
10	Picking Green
12	Travelling With A Bitter Melon
14	Images of Hong Kong
16	The Distinguished Leaves
19	**Jennifer Wong**
20	En Route
21	Myth
22	Shanghai Street
23	Cigarette Span
24	Calligraphy
26	fire
27	Affinity
28	Mother and Child

31	***Eddie Tay***
32	The Mental Life of Cities, ix.
34	The Mental Life of Cities, xx.
36	My Thought Fox
38	Room
40	Letter to My Baby Daughter Born in Hong Kong
42	My five-year-old who loves the buses and ferries
44	Childhood Games
45	Neighbours
46	A Second Language
49	***Timothy Kaiser***
50	my father-in-law at twenty
52	Still Life: Wan Chai At Night
53	Home-Cooked Meal
54	Minibus 14M
56	waiting for 107
58	girl on the bus
58	Statues
59	Hotel - Yangshuo, China
60	Morning Fugue
65	***Tammy Ho Lai-ming***
66	Tiny scissors
67	His t-shirts
68	Early spring
69	At risk
70	Where were you last night?
72	Newest, hottest, tallest, the most London
74	Tin Shui Wai
75	Languages

79	**Shirley Geok-lin Lim**
80	For a Hot City
81	A kind of paradise
82	Yau Yat Chuen
83	MTR lines
84	The Wee Man
85	A Wet Market in Hong Kong
86	Expatriate's farewell
88	Always
89	Hong Kong in Black: Festival Walk
90	The Children's Movement
92	Your Exercise Books
95	**Sarah Howe**
96	Crossing from Guangdong
100	Islands
105	Mother's Jewellery Box
109	**David McKirdy**
110	Outward Bound
111	We Chinese
112	Star Struck
114	A Red Guitar, Three Chords and the Truth
115	Bamboozled
116	Working Class God
118	Shining
119	Homecoming
120	Senior Citizen
121	Epistle to my unborn child

Leung Ping-kwan

Central

I thought you had come back to look for me!
It's just an ordinary Monday morning.
Shadows of people brush past, hurrying back to
the hubbub of the Stock Exchange, sombre
law firms, dental offices with the stench of medicine,
leaving behind for the moment the sun and the shadowy trees.

When was the last time I saw you? I clearly remembered
you wearing a black amah suit, carrying a load of sweet tangerine.
Amidst the faltering shadow of flowers, the skyscrapers were built.
Caterers carrying lunches on their heads, ringing bicycles
with kerosene cans rattling at their backs, sank into the stream of
    fancy cars
and disappeared together with an old post office building.

Wanchai

I seem to see that old staircase again with the shadows of
your body gathering form and then disappearing ahead.
Slightly panting in the dark, the dirty maps extend
across dark corners, the tatooed vernacular buildings
stained with sweat. Striding in high-slit Cheongsam, you are beautiful
and vulnerable as a new stretch of reclaimed land.

You walk down the stairs, thinking of your parents' wartime driftings.
Taps never properly turned off; the incessant tick-tock of history
keeps count of various ships coming in to anchor. You ran into a sailor
who came to the photo studio and strange questions about this
     foreign land.
After many wars, churches and dancing halls were torn down,
leaving on the wall only his naïve face frozen in a smile.

Ladder Street

It's got to be magic, old clogs in Ladder Street,
my shadow and I scraping along, down, clacking back into the years,
noting soley ankle spreading to ankle.
Clothes poles pointed to the years, their days hung out to dry.
("Clothes poles! Get your clothes poles here!")
Memory is like scissors. ("Any scissors to grind? Knives to sharpen?")
Memory cuts lots of things into silhouettes.
As I talked to myself, the moon happened to wander at my side.
When I hopscotched, my shadow jumped into strange shapes.
I slipped on my clogs and flashed on everything.

Right here in Ladder Street I almost lost them;
I slipped out of my clogs and I slipped from the spell.
How strange and ordinary, like birds disappearing in thin air.
Then modern buildings shot up, and storm clouds rolled.
I hunkered here in the concrete, felt for my shadow.
In spite of roads above and below, I heard your voice,
a jump-rope song, "the flowers bloomed then, one and ten..."
I could barely make it out for the cars.
Why can't one make appointments with bygone voices?
"Tomorrow at ten? wear the clogs; I'll hear you then."

(translated by Gordon T Osing)

An Old Colonial Building

Through sunlight and shadow dust swirls,
through the scaffolding raised-up around
the colonial edifice, over the wooden planks
men live on to tear it brick by brick, the imperial
image of it persisting right down, sometimes,
to the bitter soil in the foundation, sometimes finding, too,
the noble height of a rotunda, the wide, hollow corridors
leading sometimes to blocked places, which, sometimes,
knocked open, are stairs down to ordinary streets.

Down familiar alcoves sometimes brimming
with blooms sometimes barren I go to Xerox
glancing at the images caught in the circular pond,
now showing the round window in the cupola as the duskweed drifting,
day and night caught in the surface, no longer textbook
clean, but murky, the naïve goldfish searching
mindlessly around in it, shaking the pliant lotus stems
and the roots feeling for eatch, swirling orange and white
gills opening and leeching, in and out of the high window bars.

Might all the the pieces of ruins put together present
yet another architecture? Ridiculous the great heads on money,
laughable the straight faces of running things. We pass in this corridor
in the changing surface of the pond by chance
our reflections rippling a little. We'd rather not bend;
neither or us in love with flags or fireworks.
So what's left are these fragmentary, unrepresentative words,
not uttered amidst the buildings of chrome and glass, but beside
a circular pond riddled with patterns of moving signs.

(translated with Gordon T Osing)

Kuafu at Exchange Square

I think we all still like the story
On the escalators, I see a girl before me
running to catch the departing train
I know if I fall, there'll be no clamor
Can I change the grease stains on your clothes
into raindrops on peach leaves?
Meeting by chance, telling myth stories over lunch
we are made of imagination and clay
In this city, you head for the forest dragging a river behind
running through rough pebbles
skin calloused, gradually removed
(the traffic hurries off)
from all the warmth of the planet
The cold moon kneading the tame dough, hard
Life makes you hear noises in your head
You hold up your strong arms to catch
the halo of light, like an autumn in love
Air drafts around your waist make you shudder
You wish to bring sunflowers to those moving among the high-rises
but accumlated burdens make your steps heavy. We pass through
    the footbridge
to look at the sky and distant mountains, a metal crab
raises its large pincers in Exchange Square
as if it can gulp down a whole ocean in thirst
Like trees stubbornly fighting the dust of the world
you cast shades to shelter the fatigued
We walk along the edge of the bustling city, I think I see
the weary one falling, shaking the river on his head
sprinkling the world with fresh dew drops

Kuafu is a mythical giant from the Scroll of Mountains and Seas. *He wanted to drive away the ferocious sun to stop it from scorching people and their land, but died of fatigue and thirst before his mission was accomplished. When he dies, his hair became a river and cane turned into peach trees to quench the thirst of exhausted men and women who came after.*

Postcards of Old Hong Kong

The Pictures we sent off had been touched up
images of scenes we never experienced
                              On the back,
I'll send greetings, in that space
were I to tell my deepest anxieties and worries
would they among endless strangers circulate, before
curious or indifferent eyes, bleaching the sepia
lighter and fainter, until those old-style tea-houses in Happy Valley,
flower stalls along Lyndhurst Terrace, hawkers of all sorts,
like the old woman spinning threads at branches of trees,
gradually fade
              From mass-produced pictures
I pick and choose, wondering how to convey news of me
I don't want to sensationalise the huge fire at the race course, or
      the typhoon
that sank the cruiser in the harbour, I'm not the tourist
scribbling at the margin of a disaster scene:
"We are off to Shanghai for a jaunt!" I'm no
smart broker or colonial official, engrossed in sending home
exotica: opium smoking, long-plaited
gamblers, songstresses, Kung Fu masters, rickshaw pullers,
I flip them over, disgusted. True,
they exist, but I rather not use them to
represent us
              At the picture border I wrote
hasty words straying sometimes into Kennedy Town side streets,
the first Chinese school in Morrison Hill, the reservoir where
China-bound ambassador-laden horses stopped and drank

I've always wanted to ask how history was made
Lots of people tinted the pictures, lots of people
named the streets after themselves, statues were
put up and taken down. Amidst overflowing clichés
I wrote you a few words, crossing set
boundaries
        How do we, on gaudy pictures of the past
write words of the moment? Stuck in their midst, how we paint ourselves?

(translated by Martha Cheung)

Picking Green

A wooden plank
across a field of water.
She squats there,
picking water-cress for us.
She's good at it,
picking left and right.
In no time

she fills her bag.
Out on the plank,
she looks so small,
against the massive mountains.
Don't put your faith
in supersize plants,
she says,
don't envy the carambola,
leave it in the supermarket,
she says,
that's where it belongs

Those things will only make you sick,
if you eat them,
like black magic,
arrow-root and lotus-root,
grown to be
several times bigger than they should be;
cherry tomatoes
all dressed up in purple and red;
pumpkins turning into mountains,
injected with who knows what

She just plants
a few acres of water-cress.
Then as the seasons change
gourds and beans.
It's been warm this year,
the water-cress has ripened,
so sweet and refreshing,
it will nourish us
down to our innards

She squats on the planks,
over the water,
nimbly picking, right and left.
A whole bag
will sell for just twenty dollars,
bearing with it
the freshness and beauty
of a whole morning,
Bigger doesn't mean better,
she says.

(translated by John Minford)

Travelling With A Bitter Melon

I cooked it at noon
sliced it, then stir-fried it
It was delicious, a little biter, a little sweet
carrying the good wishes you brought with you from another place
On your way back you had it for company
It must have gradually turned tender and soft beside you
How did you carry it?
Did you check it in? Or hand-carry it?
Did it look about curiously in the plane? Did it
cry because of hunger? Did it get airsick?
I said it was raining outside, you said where you were
it was sunny, you were about to set off to my city
so you thought you could bring it with you, carry it
across different climates, different customs and manners
I believed you when I set eyes on it
thanks to you I saw its colour - so unique
In what climate and soil did it grow and from what species?
This child from a poor family has grown into a body like jade
has an endearing character, a kind of soft gentle white
not dazzling, but glowing as if from within
I took this white bitter melon with me onto the plane
and arrived at a foreign land, stepped onto foreign soil
only at the Customs did I wonder if anyone had asked you:
Why isn't it green like most bitter melons?
As they examined its dubious passport, ready to stir up trouble
the innocent newcomer waited patiently, a heavy past on his shoulders
while it remained endearing as ever, neither bitter nor sour
but gently making allowances for those overworked disgruntled
weary-eyed grim-faced immigration officials
I took it with me and went on and on, like my words, further and
further off the mark, trying harder to be inclusive

because I didn't want to leave out any details, about how a bitter melon
tossed and turned at night, missing its mates,
gasping - was it torn by memories of that
familiar place under the melon-shed, by feelings some may find trivial?
You're so kind towards my clumsy language habits, when I asked:
When will you be back? You just said:
When will you go? One leaving, one
returning. You accepted the tenses I used
Tenses slippery and imprecise. I always eat bitter melons
I ate one before I boarded the plane
Why then did it come all that way back to my table?
Did it want to tell me the bitterness of separation? of frustration?
Did it want to let me know it had a tumour? that its face
was wrinkled with loneliness?
that it kept having bad nights, kept waking in the early hours
and with open eyes waited for the arrival of dawn? In the rippling
silence, was it telling me it was illness that made it bitter?
or its inability to make whole the fragments of history?
Or was it the bitterness of being misunderstood by strangers,
of being misplaced in a hostile world?
It still looked so translucent, like white-jade
so soothing the thought of savouring it eased one's nerves
I was saying what everyone should say
expressing amidst lucid phrases what I wanted to say
in confused sentences. Alone I set the table
the ocean between us, how I yearned to be with you
and share with you the refreshing melon
There are so many things that do not live up to expectations
The human world has its imperfections
The bitter melon understands.

(translated by Martha Cheung)

Images of Hong Kong

I need a new angle
for strictly visual matters.
Here's an old portrait shot originally
in Guangguang studio in Nathan Road;
They don't paint on them like this any more.
For no reason of mine, Midlevels scenes are on the television.
She's come from unforgettable Shanghai, from glamorous
Jaffe Road, with its White Russian coffee shops, violins
playing into the night. How does it add up?
A bottle of lotion, Two Sisters, smashed forever on the floor.
Imagine the old vendors throwing olives up into a postmodern tower.
Even the old lady who knows only we're all different has a point.
Here's a man who studied anarchism in France and came home
to work for "Playboy", then "Capital".
The tiniest angles divide our views of the moon
when we look up. The Star Ferry clock-tower,
sunsets in Aberdeen: too familiar. Only now somebody plans to redo
everything. Queen's Cafe. China Club
One has only to push buttons to change pictures
to get in so many trends one can't even think,
too much trivia and so many places and stories
one can't switch identities fast enough. When can we - ?
And here's the Beijing journalist who became
an expert on pets and pornography under capitalism.
When can we just sit down and talk?
Our attentions get lost in factories of images and songs;
appetites are whetted in the hungers of the tiny screen.
Reach out and touch - what?

History, too, is a montage of images,
of paper, collectibles, plastic, fibres,
laser discs, buttons. We find ourselves looking up
at the distant moon; tonight's moon -
does it come at the beginning or the end of time?
Here's another from Taiwan, who thinks
she's Eileen Chang writing Hong Kong romances, with neon
dancing in the back-churing waters of the Star Ferry, on the old depot
with Repulse Bay Hotel rendezvous produced on cue.
All this exotic stuff, of course, is for export.
We need a fresh angle,
nothing added, nothing taken away,
always at the edge of things and between places.
Write with a different color for each voice;
OK, but how trivial can you get?
Could a whole history have been concocted like this?
Why are there so many good Oriental spy novels?
Why are there so many things that can't be said?
So now, once again, they say it's time to remodel
and each of us finds himself look around for - what?

(translated by Gordon T Osing)

The Distinguished Leaves

Noting the variety and richness of the lotus leaves
I paused at a pond to chat, and you pointed
Across the flattened sheen of their surfaces
to exalted velvet presenting a pearly bloom,
royalty disdaining all the surrounding green.
You affected surprise to find anything here worth seeing.

You favoured London on a grey evening; you recalled
strong red tea, a cold hearth, and an atmosphere
of talk os shadowy old bookshops and the precious
musty presence of antique tomes. I nodded, knowing

for several moments, past and present, words failed to explain;
then breezes stirred the leaves to sound like schoolboys
reciting in a foreign language, mumbling, garbling, indistinct.
The superior leaves swayed, sustained by all that lived beneath.

(translated by Gordon T Osing)

Leung Ping-kwan was born in Guangdong but grew up in Hong Kong. Writing in Chinese about Hong Kong life, his focus was always intensely local.

As his fame grew, he became increasingly identified as the "authentic" Hong Kong literary voice. Indeed, he was well-known for comments about how Hong Kong Chinese literature had been marginalised, both by mainland Chinese writers and scholars who could only see it as peripheral and by western readers who could not see "China" beyond the mainland. But from first to last, he remained open to literatures from different places and in different languages.

This openness was an expression of the curiosity he had about the world—the world he lived in, he travelled to, he read about. This curiosity developed texture and density as it led him to probe the details of everyday living and find in them unexpected provocations to thought. Nothing was too small or insignificant for poetry—his first medium and in many ways, his most accomplished.

Whatever he took from life for art, he also gave back: inanimate objects took on his personality, streets and scenes came alive with his hospitality; Hong Kong became once more intriguing and ever more different because he invited us to look at it in the myriad ways he did.

(adapted from commentary by Dr Elaine Ho in the Asian literary journal Cha*)*

Leung Ping-kwan's poems have been published and anthologized widely.

Jennifer Wong

En Route

Tonight she walks home
by another route,
passing a tennis court
lit by white stadium lights.

In the darkness she hears
the flutters of an owl.

She feels the hem of her skirt
brushing her knees as she walks.

She wishes for something to happen.
Anything.

Myth

Do not talk to trees.

They have deep squinting eyes
and long stout necks. Rough chafing leather.

In the warm house you feel them,
their breaths in your old furniture,

their harmless hooks and smiles
in your child's picture books.

It's hard to get lost in the woods
if you don't mean to.

Do not talk to trees.

At night they dance in ballet shoes,
tell secrets to one another,
put on a ring, wisdom for every year.

Shanghai Street

It is the missing block four of a development,
the way we avoid going outdoors
one summer evening of ghost festival.

We suspect foreigners may be confused
by shop signs that read
'Celestial Pleasures' or
'Eternal Living' nestled between
tuck-shops and stationers
in the middle of Shanghai Street.
I heard that folks went there
for quality timber and craftsmanship.

When I was a kid I used to think
they were toy shops - all those
paper houses, paper dolls,
paper shirts and even mobile phones.
I didn't know until the day I saw
Grandmother burned them after purchase.

I didn't know what to do
with the packet I received:
a coin, a sweet, and tissue paper.
A riddle.
How strange it feels,
things we don't talk about.

Cigarette Span

You roll and burn a cigarette
from beginning to end.
I watch your planet orange glow and burn.

You're safe in my train of thoughts.
I don't want more.
I'm your one-minute neighbour, friend
sharing shelter as this rain holds on.

Calligraphy

We owe our imagination to the ancient birds:
their footprints scrawled on the land.

We find fiery symbols on clay pots
in the ruins of Xian.

The jug of meanings poured
into every character.

To learn to swim
in a sea teemed with images:

four sturdy strokes stand
for the gallops of horses;

loops and spirals
that serve as fish-bodies;

to take three trees
for a forest

and to carve a shell that leans
on the back of a turtle.

You are the one better off, being ignorant.
You don't see the blade

above my heart; can't feel
sadness has to do with autumn,

or a character in my name spells
rain cloud over a field;

but our parting's been told
in the sky-scattering of birds.

fire

My five elements.
The flowers of hero trees.
The gravity of earth and history.
A red boiled egg on my birthday.
The red bit in my Chunghwa pencil.
The language of protest
runs in my body, flows in my blood.
The explosion of the fire crackers.
I dream the Dream of the Red Chamber.
I drink the red sorghum wine.
Five bright stars shine on the red carpet.
A white bauhinia grows on the same red.
Red is our metaphor. Look at the red baby
of Zhang Xiao Gang. Look. Look.
You never forget.
The red lanterns sway in the dark.
Even in my sleep, the red blood flows.

Affinity

Yesterday, an old friend came to visit me,
And we talked and talked
To the beat of the pop songs.
Then, suddenly, in the middle of the sentence,
Interrupting me and the radio,
He said, "Do you have a Chinese album here?"
And I asked,
"Why?"
He replied, "Just put it on."

Today, through the sunny window
Below my balcony,
A brown and a black bob
Are conversing in a foreign tongue -
The surrounding English brick walls regurgitate
All the echoes and the vowels.
Somehow their voices penetrate me,
Send forth
A sense of affinity
That I can understand.

This, or maybe not only this
Stirs memory, like dust motes in the air.
I remember the way my mother used to talk to me
And then suddenly,
The sunspot on the window
Blurs.

Mother and Child

You showed me how to tell
a fresh egg by its shell,
holding it up against the lamp.

You'd look up at the sky, predict
from the stillness of the air
when the rain would arrive.

The language of your dishes:
ginger and tangerine peel julienned
to the finest; fish steamed to perfection.

On long summer nights
you'd lull me to sleep
in the breeze of your palm leaf fan.

Even caning, when it happened,
was a way of loving despite the hurt.
It has made me a braver girl.

And that first time I stood on the swing,
facing the wind, flying forward,
seeing the world with your help,

leaving but not leaving you.

Born and raised in Hong Kong, **Jennifer Wong** attended Diocesan Girls' School and, as a Swire scholar, studied English at Oxford. Now residing in Britain pursuing a PhD in poetry, she is a poet, copy-writer, researcher and translator. In 2014, she received the Young Artist Award (Literary Arts) from the Hong Kong Arts Development Council.

"The modern city of Hong Kong with its crowd of lingerie departments, coffee, Xerox machines and stilettos, merges into the voices of ancient and modern China in a set of fine translations..." said the poet George Szirtes of these poems. And Michael Ingham wrote: "While Jennifer Wong's voice reveals respect for and understanding of the city's Chinese heritage, it also speaks passionately of our city's cultural hybridity and fusion."

The poems that appear were selected from her two collections published by Chameleon Press: *Goldfish* and *Summer Cicadas*.

Eddie Tay

The Mental Life of Cities, ix.

Cantonese is cunning, is cunning;
in the city's concrete, vowels crack and widen.

In August heat, smog rises
like fists from factories and I wonder
if it is possible to model stanzas
on stained buildings in Mongkok.

There are runaway hexameters
coursing through veins of street protesters,
rainwater rhymes from shopkeepers
and sharp syllables from sweaty bankers.

I wonder if it is possible to thread syllables
through lines of red and green taxis.

The shopkeeper says no with his glance,
the men in business suits at Central say no;
the boutique women say no:
a person hiding away for hours, days, years,
doing his own thing, coaxing images
that tumble wet and blue onto pages
has no credit, is not good for business.

Cantonese is cunning, is cunning;
in the city's concrete, vowels crack and widen.

In winter there is a rhythm
along hiking trails; stones are themes
we have to learn to read. Leaves are forgotten
and green turns abstract and fades.

Do we remember? Can we try? I wonder
if it is possible to thread syllables through lines
of red and green taxis. The shopkeeper says no
with his glance, the men in business suits at Central
say no; the boutique women say no.

Cantonese is cunning, is cunning;
in the city's concrete, vowels crack and widen.

The Mental Life of Cities, xx.

Year after year
concrete refuses
to return to the soil.

Some stay quiet
on village paths.

Others break
from being stepped upon too often
and migrate.

Some go on the internet
and hide with pseudonyms.

And still others remain stubborn and protest
about bridges, piers, clock towers,
about visas and work permits given
to the wrong kind of concrete.

Nobody listens to concrete.

Under the sun,
concrete pretends.

Most concrete is employable.

It is the post-1980s concrete.

Under the moon,
concrete shrinks, cracks and returns
to a changed pavement
under the flagpole
with the stars.

My Thought Fox

Finally, three a.m.,
sloughing off a cold and headache,
I am fresh from sleeping
at eight in the evening,
waiting for a thought fox.

A bottle of milk is ready
on the table next to the baby cot
as she needs to feed
on a four-hourly basis.

In this shoebox of an apartment
I look at the characters with *pinyin*
pasted on the door:
口, 手, 鼻, 眼, 腳, 耳。　　　Mouth, hand, nose, eye, foot, ear.

It is my wife's idea,
and I hope my son's Chinese
will be better than mine.

My thought fox will not arrive.

On the dining table
are my son's leftover cookies.

His school bag, bright red,
lies on its side in the middle
of the living room: the crayons
and jotter book spill
like a car wreck.

It is eleven degrees Celsius,
a Hong Kong winter,
and I am a snail in its shell.

I google Ted Hughes,
scan his poem online for inspiration,
and read the latest on Obama.

My thought fox will not arrive.

I check my e-mail.

I hear cooing and sighing -
my baby is awake.

Room

When I think everyone's asleep,
I sketch a room out of "corner",
"wall", "door" and enter.

I write "window",
paste it on the wall
and look out.

There is a green cottage
halfway up a blue hill,
a unicorn waiting by the gate.

I scribble "road" and "pavement"
and lift a foot, about to climb
through the window,

when my baby daughter starts to cry
in the other room,
the one I forgot.

I went for the door
and left one room for another
to cradle her in my arms.

I have lost
the green cottage, the blue hill
the unicorn.

Wherever I go, I will always return
to this city of buses and ferries,
pollution and factories.

I will find on the thirty-eighth floor
a cramped flat with a pink room,
a pink cot and my daughter.

Perhaps these are my green cottage,
my blue hill,
my unicorn.

Letter to My Baby Daughter Born in Hong Kong

My dear Tabitha: when I first heard your cries while clasping
    your mother's hand I knew I had done this right, that you
    are beautiful and perfect like Christ. I was thinking, as you
    emerged wet, warm and slightly blue from that other world,
    I hope you will find this cauldron of a city good enough, that
    your father and mother are good enough.
I know you will grow to know this city, know its ferries chugging
    onward and mini-buses gunning forward into the future
    of economists and governments. You will swim in the
    Cantonese of shopkeepers and know the Mandarin of
    tourists. You will get to know Titus, your older brother, who
    picks up Cantonese like noodles on chopsticks, though
    sometimes he receives curious looks from those in *cha
    chaan tengs* unused to a boy speaking fluent English. Maybe
    you will never know how foreign this feels to me. When
    I first arrived, I couldn't understand those pushy elbows
    and shoulders in the MTR. And what kind of abbreviation
    is "MTR" anyway? I kept thinking that the "R" had been
    misplaced. I may have to remind you, until you see it for
    yourself, that in Singapore, the subway is called the MRT.
    Singapore and Hong Kong are to mummy and daddy what
    Hong Kong and Singapore will be to both of you. I can't help
    but think I'll lose you to Hong Kong, the way I am losing
    Titus, who no longer talks about the MRT the way he used
    to back in Singapore. You might grow up thinking that the
    MRT in Singapore is the subway with its "R" misplaced.

Here we are in a flat on the thirty-eighth floor above a congested shopping mall on a summer morning. You're wrapped up like a bean and squirming and we're ready to take you to the clinic for a routine check-up. But nothing is routine from the first day - from the exhaustion of your mother like a crumpled leaf from cradling you all night, the rhythms of your breath like tides of the sea, your skin the colour of pre-dawn sky, to the groaning traffic while we're in a red taxi, that unfurling slope down from the hospital past sweltering neighbourhood estates when we first brought you back home - these are important, just as your first words will be rainfall on parched skin.

Sometimes I think it is impossible to write poetry in such a cauldron of a city. Every morning I carry a briefcase. I count the numbers above lift doors with my neighbours. I smile and frown at the stock market. I have learnt joys and sorrows from business pages of newspapers. I am afraid I will fall asleep and let this poem disappear with me. But you are my poems oh my children, my works in progress, controllable and out of control. I know that cliché about how we're dying the moment we're born, but I feel as if I am awake once again.

My five-year-old who loves the buses and ferries

At a poetry reading, someone asked.
I looked away and read something I wrote years ago.
I went home and became a parent,
trying not to be a ghost
to my five-year-old who loves the buses and ferries
of this city, who says:
Daddy daddy hold on tightly now
I want to hang upside down.

From the stalls of Mongkok
to boutiques at Central,
the Christmas of this city kept me sane,
and I thought of Red Pine and his bare feet
who spoke of hermits and Buddhism
in ancient China at a gathering of wine lovers.
And I thought of my five-year-old
who loves the buses and ferries
of this city, who says:
Once upon a time there was an old lady
who stepped on my pencil.

I watched a documentary
about Ko Un, made honorary citizen
in a town in Italy, and I wonder
if my poem would travel
when I'm a father.
And I thought of my five-year-old
who loves the buses and ferries
of this city, who says: *Mm goi, mm goi,*
I want you to read Hansel and Gretel
and the sweet house.

These are fragments, my friends.
I am trying for a soliloquy
among savvy business people
and neon lights, though all the time
I'm thinking of dinner at home,
of my five-year-old who loves the buses and ferries
of this city, who says:
Daddy, daddy, you're writing again
I want your pen for ABC's
now and I'm counting
一二三, 一二三四五。   One two three, one two three four five.

Childhood Games

At the corridor
we mimicked pugilists, cops and robbers,
secretly tried five-stones (a girls' game),
drew lines on concrete floor and played hopscotch.
two were on your team, three on mine. You cried
foul play and swore never to speak to me.

During a blackout, I revealed a pack of Cat's Eyes.
We swore brotherhood, etching characters,
solemnising vows in the air. You singed my shorts
and mother was furious. At Mid-Autumn Festival,
I held a plastic lantern. You looked down
at your flammable trifle.

Father wanted to move house.
Be happy, at least we can afford to upgrade,
look at Ah Teck they all, sure cannot make it.
He installed a computer. I forgot our games,
met new neighbours. Su-yin attends ballet classes.
Peter plays the piano and detests rough play.

Sometimes, I gaze along the corridor,
in case I am not alone.

Neighbours

Another pair of feet shuffles
along the corridor. A dog barks,
some kids cry mum, it is the same
TV programme we watch. We do not
want to hear what they see. These walls
are too thin, so do not invade their privacy.

Ours is enough. Pretend, play the game,
avert glances if we meet. Rattle metal grills,
or clink, clink, clink our keys to conceal.
We need not peek through window panes
to know where they are, what they do.
We have our lives. In the mornings,
we curse silently at their alarm clocks.

But to acknowledge this is to break
the courtesy of our understanding.

A Second Language

But I have never read proverbs on bamboo,
never felt the flourish of my name
in Chinese characters with the grip
and stroke of a brush. No calligraphy
records my genealogy. I know nothing,

Though I recognise grandfather's face,
and recognise his father's face peering
from dusty portraits, and his father's
father's from a history book that records
my people flocking from a farther land.

My Mandarin becomes a second language
that fades like the memory of an old textbook.
I am familiar with only the Word and Cross
while yin and yang become superstition
just as herbs for wind are old wives' tales.

So now I study Chinese history
in English, commanding a feeble tongue
with the aid of *han yu pin yin*, imitating
melodious inflections, like a child learning
ABC's.

Eddie Tay's poetry is a reflection of the postcolonial realities of Hong Kong and Singapore. As a Singaporean Chinese writing in English and teaching poetry and creative writing at the Department of English in the Chinese University of Hong Kong, his work is a result of the interpenetration of languages and cultures in which he lives.

"Poetry," he says, "isn't only about your grasp of the language; it's about life and your feelings. As long as you feel, you can write. In Hong Kong, English is a pragmatic language. It's a tool, but I try to show my students that it's also a medium of thinking and feeling, one that has to do with their cultural identity."

His collection *The Mental Life of Cities*, from which these poems are taken, was published by Chameleon Press and won the Singapore Literature Prize 2012.

Timothy Kaiser

my father-in-law at twenty

when mother-in-law goes to the mainland
for a few days
father-in-law will take off his shirt
unwire the ancestral wok from the ancestral nail
mix salt and steam and cigarette ash into the fried rice
he learned to make in London.

in London when he was twenty
standing by a snowy statue in Trafalgar Square
someone taking black and white snapshots of him
wearing an impressive white woman
in an expensive white hat.

he handsome in a dark suit
speaking dishwasher English yet
the way he holds his cigarette
the way he leans towards her
dismisses the camera the cold
the woman must have understood.

I have seen those pictures
my wife knows where they are hidden
and he once told me when others were in bed
how on the ship from Hong Kong to London
there was more than one fistfight with *gwei lo*
except when the ship stopped in Egypt
a ceasefire to see the Sphinx
he has lost the photos, he says,
smiling
coughing
checking his heart
blowing smoke away from me,
too long ago.

for my father-in-law at twenty
the sands of Egypt spicy under his feet
fists bloodied against condescension
stacks of unwashed dishes awaiting his arrival in London
and a mysterious white woman
smiling at him from under an expensive white hat
the riddles of the Sphinx must once have seemed
no more difficult than striking a match
on ice.

Still Life: Wan Chai At Night

rentgirl massages her spine against the railing
blows nicotine bubbles at a star
runs a painted finger up the slit of her skirt
an itch
her job is to ignore the bald spot
and accept everything including American Express
young
eager
cable TV pushers
from cable TV's mean streets
peddle their nocturnal 2-D narcotic
retreat back into the shadows
when backpackers and American sailors feign broken antennae
a drunken businessman
the world his urinal
tries to do up his belt
beside a beggar
limbs swallowed by sidewalk
neither of them notice
the black moths nibbling at their fabric.

Home-Cooked Meal

5 a.m. cigarette
morning brand of the sun
makes fish taste better
    aaaaah . . . much better

one magnificent fish
hooked as Central banker son knots his good morning tie
slaps on his face a foreign scent
    ha ha

one puny bottom feeder with tiger shark dreams
grandson will want for a pet
show to all his friends
This is the fish my grandpa caught
This is the fish my grandpa caught
All on a Monday morning.
    damn

there was a time
could feed the whole village
and the village dogs
and the village gods

now all
it seems
including the fish
prefer breakfast combos
at McDonald's

Minibus 14M

Thirty-two years ago,
in Driver Yip's Form 4 English class,
Madame Chang,
bloodhound of a teacher,
death on the trail of an unsharpened pencil,
hobbled homework,
asked for submission of a mystery,
at least 300 words,
double-spaced,
by Wednesday.

Thirty-two years ago,
for Madame Chang's 300-word mystery,
all Driver Yip could think of
was how one evening,
his mother,
three years before,
had cut fruit into delicate sailboats,
removed the seeds,
the next morning was removed from her sheets,
and how his father had had nothing to say,
and neither had Driver Yip,
even after the cane scorched his skin,
and Madame Chang cleared her throat,
polished her glasses,
said something about 'lazy boys',
but then closed the door softly.

Driver Yip hopes Madame Chang,
if not dead,
hunched over a cane,
will admire his neat English letters
in his notice to all passengers of minibus 14M:
> advise the new fare - $3.80 please
> sorry no change
> thank you, your kindness attention.

for his mother, Driver Yip has glued on the dashboard
pink and gold plastic prayerwheels,
an antique miniature doll astride a tiny wooden horse,
a golden Buddha,
eyes unblinking,
blessing sailboats adrift inside an air freshener bottle
of the bluest sea.

for Driver Yip's father, a cactus,
lashed by wire to the passenger side air vent,
that blooms once every year
as Driver Yip steers down the mountain.
he cannot bring himself to water it.
he cannot bring himself to throw it away.

waiting for 107

pissed off because
the bus I'm supposed to take
the 107
the bus I've been waiting over 20 minutes for
the 107
and it's drizzling now
is not the bus pulling up right now
it's the 95B
B for Bastard

the last passenger to get off
a woman
alights ever

so

slowly
B for Bloody Hell
I hunt for my umbrella as the bus
scoffs away from the curb
enveloping us in its indifference
the woman who got off last stands and digs in her purse for her
    umbrella
ever

so

slowly
unfolds it
digs again for a cane
unfolds it

B for Blind?

she taps by me
and I watch as she is dammed by sidewalk renovations
then trickles through each barricade

it's raining harder now
but I keep my umbrella unfolded
my eyes unopened
as I try to guess what a 107 sounds like
what a 107 sounds like
while the rain taps against my soul.

girl on the bus

there is a special face
flashed by Hong Kong girls:
quarter pout, quarter puppy, quarter cobra, quarter coquette.
a girl is practising these proportions
with the window
in the seat ahead of me.
just when she has it right
she notices me
for real.

Statues

In a world carved
by statues
the Venus on the train
platform
texts my eyes
before chiselling herself
into her phone.

Hotel - Yangshuo, China

clocks behind the dusty desk give time for
New York, London, Tokyo
but what time is it here?
the carpet says 1967
give or take a revolution.
granite pillow promises quarry dreams
across the street a dai pai dong circus
three doors down the promiscuous mating of mah jong tiles
around my head a convention of dentist mosquitos
lining up for the buffet
only the nightwatchman will sleep tonight.
on the ceiling tiles above me
I can make out the map of my youth
the legend says there is a paradise
at 3 a.m. I am still searching.

Morning Fugue

Squished next to me on the KCR is a girl
In her delicately pressed school uniform
Practising piano on the palm of her left hand
Fingers prancing
Pawing as we reach each station.
Eyes closed, she does not see me mount the podium
    Clear my throat
    Raise my arms
    Frown bemusedly
With an odd swelling of sympathy and annoyance
At the musicians from the mainland
Looking bewildered by so many puzzling notes,
Their strings encased in blue, red, and white.
    Point accusingly my Octopus at the timpani player
Or was that unpleasantry from the euphonium section?
    Suck sharply my air
At the swaying violinist
Jabbing her Stradivarius
Into my back.

Those early enough to find a seat
Do not notice our performance
It being a Wednesday
Audience rustling and readying themselves
With the score and pedigree
Of Happy Valley's 1st through 7th movements.

Out of nowhere, strains of Beethoven performed by a solo horn
Yet everyone reaches for their phones
I turn to the prodigy in her delicately pressed school uniform
Apologies towering high on my shoulders
FOR ALL THE IMPERTINENCE.

Vanished
Among the alighters in Kowloon Tong.

Timothy Kaiser, whose day job is with the Canadian International School of Hong Kong, was born in Iowa and grew up in the rugged mountains of northwest British Columbia and on the plains of wheatbelt Saskatchewan, Canada.

His wife, Teri, is from a Hakka village in the New Territories of Hong Kong. They lived with her family during his first years in Hong Kong and village life is represented in many of his poems.

"Kaiser does what a poet should do in his community," wrote a reviewer. "He gives voice to life within it, whether good or bad. He speaks for many of Hong Kong's people, permanent and transient."

These poems come from *Food Court*, published by Chameleon Press, except for "Statues", which is a more recent work.

Tammy Ho Lai-ming

五

Tiny scissors

Her tiny scissors, sharpened in the morning,
were dull again by the time
she acted hostess and set two mahjong tables,
side by side, in her cramped living room.

Like her mother before her, she used
the scissors to cut food into small pieces.
Toothless, gums eroded like seaside rocks,
eating was not enjoyed, only endured.

She never learnt Cantonese, despite
living in Hong Kong most her life.
She held the belief that Hakka, if uttered slowly,
would be universally understood.

Her eldest granddaughter, I was the one
for whom nothing was misunderstood.
In the last week, she gave me her scissors,
and reminded me that I'd too one day be toothless.

His t-shirts

Medium-sized t-shirts on his dark body.
He's totally Chinese - more so than me.
But in periods when he's building bridges,
fixing window panes or drilling roads,
I think he's from Africa.
Yellow skin is black in the sun.
Who said colours are God-given?

Medium-sized t-shirts he has aplenty.
Elated, in countries foreign, we do not forget
at home he's suppressing his worried lips.
He wants nothing from us, but
we like the idea of giving. And so he's
wearing t-shirts from London, Thailand,
Auckland, Japan, Finland, India,
Malaysia, Poland, Korea...
'Where are you from, father?' We are
teasers. Names of places bold
in English on his chest. He doesn't know.
'China,' he answers. We laugh.
We laugh. Bad daughters.

Medium-sized t-shirts on top of Large
-sized ones in his drawers.
He once stood huge
in front of a snack bar,
buying us coca-colas,
and we cheered.

Early spring

Early Spring,
the weather is still cool.
Together, in the garden
so fresh with morning air,
we make a mud model of you
with your stubborn chin
and one of me
with eyes in the shape of
almonds.

But I break the models
into hundreds of pieces,
provoked by I know not what -
sometimes my mood swings;
more violent than a tightened
string.

Without a word you gently mix
the broken pieces of us
with water. Your tenderness
surprises me; and once
again you make a model of you
and a model of me.

Now there's me in you,
and you in me.

    Based on a Chinese poem by Sanmao.

At risk

And so it is true.
My shoes are torn and my toes show.
I'm not worried about the toe nails:
Long, hard. They follow nature's law.

People have already noticed me.
An unwanted street decoration.
I see from here where I squat
The sky is dimmed too early,
And children gather to eat ice-cream,
Their fingers chubby, neglectful, white.
I am vacant. They are full.

Listen! Are they gone? Now, the wind.
The wind is movement of air.
It is reciting something. You must believe me.
It recites people's secrets, sex, memories.
I don't want to know.

Tonight, I won't sleep, to match the stars.
And I pray for a quiet night.
Don't send me rain, don't send me men,
Don't send me rhythms or a dirty hand.
Don't.

Where were you last night?
for Steven Digman

Where were you last night?
In the city centre. At a book launch.
The writers read too long, the microphones
were loud.
I drank some wine, didn't eat.
I wanted to smash those piles of books.
They looked too neat.

Where were you last night?
In the woods, catching unicorns.
The white rabbit guided me.
Fireflies danced with dying bees.
I laid a deer next to her mother
where there was scent of cedarwood.
I watched them fall into a deep deep sleep.
Were you the hawk across the great lake?
Your eyes kept me awake.

Where were you last night?
Waiting, in a pumpkin chariot, to be rescued.
Waiting, combing my hair in a castle,
to be rescued.
Waiting, in a Danish river, to be rescued.
Waiting, in a picture, to be rescued.
Waiting, in a glass coffin watched by dwarfs,
to be rescued.

Where were you last night?
In mourning. In the rain. Behind walls.
On a diet. On the game. In treatment. In love.
In denial. In arrears. In tears. In dependence.
In light of. In Fidel. In the right place.
In the mood. Over the moon.
Under the knife. In my mother's body.
Coming into being. Elsewhere.

Where were you last night?
Moscow. It was snowing. The flakes on my
face were hotter
than burning coals. The snow was hotter
than your worst fever. A snowflake fell
in my eye -
I have lost sight forever.

Where were you last night?
In the Chelsea hotel, standing for one night.
The man whose name I don't remember did not snore
for we didn't sleep. He whispered Mina
whenever he thought it was appropriate.
In the pub, I had given him my friend's name.
He said he liked my shoes;
they reminded him of his piano teacher.
He was ten. She was thirty-two.

Where were you last night?
At home. In my own arms. Home is my own arms.
My own arms.

Newest, hottest, tallest, the most London

You are my newest boyfriend
(the hottest, the tallest, the most
London) who is now in France.

You told me in an email (written in
haste, in an internet café):
Last Friday you spent three hours
on a bicycle. You put my photos
on the wheels; and I was travelling
with you. Crazy curly-haired you.

You liked the red ones.
You said I was at once like a playful
angel and a shameless whore.
(I deplore the comparison!
I'm only an innocent girl.)

When you stopped by the Seine,
some Parisians, mostly females, you said,
asked if they could buy my
photos. They took you as an artist
(a photographer?)
lost in paradise. 'No, no, no,' you said. 'The
photos aren't for sale.
My girlfriend is mine.'

Am I already?
Your girlfriend? Yours?

Then, you're my newest boyfriend
(the hottest, the tallest, the most
London) who is now in France.

Tin Shui Wai

Middle-aged men, now unemployed,
gather in parks and watch older men
play chess. They say they feel guilty
for not bringing money home.

Divorced women on the bus talk
about taking whole-day bus rides
to while away time and how it's better
than being alone at home, facing four walls.

Grannies who have outlived their husbands
and put their hair permanently in buns
sit on a wooden bench and ask me:
'Who are you waiting for?
Why are you so thin?'

Languages

South China Morning Post, an English newspaper, is delivered
To our doorstep every morning, and we let it
Stay until all other neighbours know
Our language abilities.
We dress well, even when taking out
The garbage or buying a San Miguel
From the store downstairs.
But let's not boast to our neighbours
How much more beautiful we are,
How much more intellectually-trained.

>They don't care. They live less ambiguously. They speak
>One dialect only. Already they are free
>From feeling embarrassed when pronouncing
>/r/ as /l/, /n/ as /l/ or /z/ as /s/. They don't feel
>Excluded when two real English speakers
>Are in the same room, commenting on
>*Memoirs of A Geisha* or
>Bill Ashcroft's postcolonial theories.
>We dare not open our mouths, lest our strong HK
>Accent betrays our humble origin. The terrible
>Flatness of our tone, the inflexibility of our tongue.

Tammy Ho Lai-Ming grew up in Hong Kong and attended the University of Hong Kong. After further studies in Britain, she returned to teach English literature at Baptist University. She is also a founding co-editor of *Cha: An Asian Literary Journal*, a leading Hong Kong-based literary journal.

Tammy Ho's first collection of poetry *Hula Hooping*, from which these poems have been selected, was fifteen years between pen and press. The poems, cross-cultural and personal, paint a broad canvas from love to language, and family to politics.

Described as "a poet of tough love, tough being and with language powerful enough to match all that," Tammy Ho is also known to see "the beauty in all things, people and moments, and this beauty—in which the personal takes in the whole world—is what she celebrates in her poetry."

Shirley Geok-lin Lim

For a Hot City
(*The Ice Rink, Festival Walk*)

For a hot city, the chill that rises
through steel and leather to feet and calves
settles in the chest like a coin, like calm,
a small hard glitter; like that which is moon,
welcomed, gazed at, desired night and day.
Twirling and spinning, circling and weaving,
arms stretch to welcome the wind's success,
unceasing rush. Silent few on the ice field
early, and later, bedlam of bodies
backsliding, shrieks like torment rising
from flames: such is this city, when freed
from burning stone and summer fire, such
the moments when it whirls delirious,
in love with the cold coin that inflames like heat.

A kind of paradise

Carefully she buttons the brand-
new checked shirt over
the sky-blue tee that sculpts the torso
in hard abs, and slips one arm
through the sleeve to be angled
in a social gesture.
A row of naked white plastics
wait to be dressed, detached
legs and arms lain on the floor,
in the bright colors of a spring
delayed by smog blown in
from the factories that color
and print the cloth that will costume
us as it now costumes this mannequin -
eyeless, in a kind of paradise.

Yau Yat Chuen
(from a poem by Song Dynasty poet Lu You, 1125-1210 AD)

in Cantonese, yet another city
of hope among a history
of cities glimmering in distances
today easily covered in glances
of hours. Presence and the present
one and the same, what can Time spend
now in this re-vision re-made stone
and glass? Excreted, yesterdays gone,
and tomorrow creeps like a slow
gas through its vents. Here, now,
is our Fate's present, to be unwrapped
each day, like Penelope unwrapped
her woven skeins, like these women
unwrap and empty bags, boxes, bins,
purses, the things that take in
and carry, like they have taken in
men, sons, in-laws, misery and story,
carrying them to yet another city
of stone and glass, to walk
in another dream festival
where tomorrow will always be today.

MTR lines

The MTR people-car stinks of afternoon
ambition fatigue and shopping zeal,
its machine air unable to sooth
the mouths sour at sucking this acidic
crush, the lemonade we do not recall
paying for. A young woman with the wide
freckled face of a Fujian farmer,
my stepmother's when she undertook
my middle-aged father's bed, smiles, pushed,
is pushed through the bodies too tightly
jammed, like his children marinated
in the short line of his life. This is the line
I stood on, inescapable, pressing
stiff shoulders among other lines
pouring out of the broken dam of China:
blood or step, Hong Kong Yan, Mainlander
or foreign-us, all the stuff of dreams waiting
to happen before the doors will open.

The Wee Man

The stroller sits by the steel polished bench.
Between the Poh Poh and helper
the boy barely standing places his pudgy
fingers to steady himself. The helper
holds a bowl of cereal in one hand,
her other in the air to catch his fall,
and Poh Poh gazes at the sippy cup
from where will come the good years, all
his manhood, the meaning of her life.
He acknowledges nothing: the helper
who will leave, home unknown; grandmother
who nourished him when he was his mother.
Three women guard the wee man standing
for the first time, the rail imprinting
its smooth steel on his soft hands.

A Wet Market in Hong Kong

No one sits in your aisles or calls you home. Scales and feathers, pink blood from a gutted fish, fresh blood from a pig split neck to anus. No one protests the violence we eat in this staging of fluorescence and narrow concrete. The ducks shine rich brown soy, the ribs are caramelized, and the cleaver smashes through bone like a tank through soft humans. I walk carefully, legs spotted by vegetable-rot puddles, pressed between baskets of yellow-blossomed choy sum and kai lan dark with chlorophyll. The young ginger roots blush translucently among gnarly turnips and pimpled potatoes, crowded among the hems of grannies poking at the flapping wings of the beheaded old hen, appraising the bright maw of a snapper that was gasping just a second ago. Like the black-robed sisters holding their scissors, snipping the threads that bind babies to their Mother Earth, mothers to children sleeping a room away, Time and its books open onto the wet market of cut green and slaughtered flesh the grannies and their families' families will eat for dinner. I enter a child and leave you a granny, hurrying into the Hong Kong humid afternoon, soles slippery with the gore of fieldairwater, migraine blinded, to sit, writing patiently, with my sisters and their scissors.

Expatriate's farewell

Goodbye to the MTR and KCR
trekking under the South China Sea, cars
emerging in the ramshackle cram
of Tai Po Market, doors opening like shazzam!
to eject citizens and their occupiers
bristling with the purses of tunnel sightseers.
Goodbye to Euro class, dreams of America,
China discounted and traders counting Bauhinia
coins equal to crowned heads of other lands.
Goodbye to pastries of sugared beans—stands
of green, yellow, red—and pastes of sesame,
lotus, thousand-year old eggs for the millennia
children of big eaters for whom every
banquet table has been reserved. Goodbye
to girls in white and blue uniforms who study
this morning's moment on mall benches,
luckier than little girls walking breakfastless
to school.   Goodbye to Ah Kongs and Ah Pohs,
bureaucrats and minor administrators,
white and black costumed waiters who never snitch
about kitchen disasters and tainted veg.

Goodbye to crayfish and shrimp waving in tanks,
to pulsing grouper, scallops and snails, the banks
of fat octopi and Alaskan crabs, perch
and snappers crowded, to be scooped and poached,
steamed or fried, for giant mouths with sharp teeth
and flowing salivary glands. Goodbye to Steve
and Jack and Martha and Pauline and Rodney,
and other peripatetic lives afloat in the bitter sea
with the sampans and Tanka fishing boats,
forever guests of this or that, and hosts
to other passing life forms. Goodbye to excess
and speed and too much is not enough, less
is never more: deep loves of transients' truths.

Always
(Hong Kong, 3 a.m.)

It is always dark before the dawn, the sleepless say.
It is always dawn before the dark, the ghost story goes.
It is always before the dark and dawn, Scripture tells.
Before it is dawn, always the dark, the elders warn.
Before always, it is the dark dawn, the poet writes.
Before dark, is it the always dawn, the children ask.
Always is the dawn, dark before it, they sing.

Hong Kong in Black: Festival Walk
(October 3, 2014)

The eye reverts this morning
To black: total curtain call?
Funereal grief? Skies tumbling

Thunder and bolts that blind
And light the cleared center?
Drop-dead fatigue behind

Security lines? Black garment bags
Bearing canisters, batons, bullets,
The BS of violence? The eye lags,

Half-asleep, among the other blacks
Who, waking, silently have dressed
For school and work, who walk

As if this morning is everyday,
Swaddled in black tees, shorts, shirts,
Yellow twists safety-pinned to say:

You're Hong Kong born-again,
Knowing finally who you are,
Subject, not subordinate slain,

Nothing's been lost. And I now awake
Am also risen to the beauty of black.

The Children's Movement
("I'm here because I love Hong Kong," at the protests, 30 Sept. 2014)

You are nine, or eleven, or perhaps
Thirteen or sixteen. In all your years
You've obeyed father and mother,
Pushing your questions down, each day
Deeper, into a dungeon of your making.
Each year has brought you new sweets,
Gifted for your tray full of past years'
Treats, many untasted, paid for you know
With father's gloom, mother's patient smiles.
And it is they you love, not the tray
That keeps you company in your room
In their absence: obedience is love,
Love obedience.
                Until that flash
Lit up their absence, and another
Briefly, clearly showed the contours
Of your dungeon in which your questions
Have crouched like rats growing larger,
Fiercer the longer unfed.

And the eighty-seven flashes
Illuminated, brighter than neon,
A radiation imprinted on your retina
To rival the lights from thousands
Of smartphones, an intelligence
Of injustice, a lesson that pierced
First your mind, penetrating
The brain's protective tough membrane
As with an x-ray dye; then, changing
The equations that regulated the universe,
Your deep heart's core, and you see, you see,
Love is disobedience, disobedience love,
And the dungeon doors open for you
and your questions to walk through.

Your Exercise Books
(for my students)

What are a few days in the Book of Changes?
Not even a blot in an exercise book,
The first stroke of a child the first time
He holds a brush wet with the black dissolved
From the ink slab, bowing before the years
Of obedience, extending his wrist to
The calligraphy of his people, more
Poetical than any other human language.
What are a few days in a student's years,
Reciting lines assigned, bowing hungry
Before the test pages passing like stale sushi
Circling endlessly in a nightmare counter?
What are a few nights of bad and good dreams
Wafting like joss the grannies light
For superior grades, smoke to mingle
With the temple soot from other grannies
Now lying in unvisited graves?
What are a few drifts of incense in the gas clouds
Condensed in the tears of children who had not known
They were warriors? What are these few days
In the children's exercise books
Blotted thick with the tears of this learning?

Shirley Geok-lin Lim is a Malaysian-Singaporean-Hong Kong-American writer, winner of the Commonwealth Poetry Prize, who sometimes believes she has her life only in language. She has three new collections out in 2015: *Do You Live In?*, *Ars Poetica for the Day*, and *The Irreversible Sun*, as well as another ten books and chapbooks of poetry published from 1980 onwards.

   She has been writing poems since nine or ten, but notes she's read many more than she has written. Poems for her "live in the memory long after their poets have passed, and it's memory's ink I look to write with. Memory throbs with beauty, which is discoverable everywhere, and pain, which is always identified with a local place, and with things glimpsed for the first time and those given up forever. The poem's music in the ear, its lyrics in the mouth, its shape on the page, its interruption in the room, its jolt on the heart: I desire these in my poems just as they attend the poems I remember."

These poems are taken from her new collection *Do You Live In?*, published by Ethos Books.

Sarah Howe

Two fingers brace the pliant spine, the thumb
at the edge - an angle exact as a violinist's
wrist - fanning through stamps to halt at the last
laminated side. He lifts his eyes to read
my face. They flicker his uncertainty
as he makes out eyes, the contour of a nose:
half-recognition. These bare moments -
something like finding family.
The mild waitress in Beijing. *Your mother . . .
China . . . worker?* she asked, at last, after
many whispers spilling from the kitchen.
Or the old woman on the Datong bus,
doubtless just inviting a foreigner to dinner,
but who could have been my unknown
grandmother, for all I knew or understood.
She took a look at me and reached up
to grasp my shoulders, loosing a string
of frantic, happy syllables, in what
dialect I don't even know. She held my
awkward hands, cupped in her earthenware
palms, until the general restlessness showed
we neared the stop. As the doors lurched open,
she smiled, pressed a folded piece of paper,
blue biro, spidery signs, between my fingers,
then joined in the procession shuffling off. Some,
I realised then, were in hard hats, as they
dwindled across the empty plain, shadowed
by the blackened, soaring, towers of the mine.

*

Something sets us looking for a place.
Old stories tell that if we could only
get there, all distances would be erased.
Wheels brace themselves against the ground
and we are on our way. Soon we will reach
the fragrant city. The island rising
into mist, where silver towers forest
the invisible mountain, across that small
span of cerulean sea. I have made
the crossing. The same journey you, a screaming
baby, made, a piercing note among grey,
huddled shapes, some time in nineteen-forty-
nine (or year one of the fledgling People's
State). And what has changed? The near-empty
bus says enough. And so, as we approach,
stop-start, by land, that once familiar scene -
the warm, pthalo-green, South China tide -
I can make out rising mercury
pin-tips, distinct against the blue
as the outspread primaries at the edge
of a bird's extending wing. So much
taller now than when I left
fifteen years ago. Suddenly, I know -
from the Mid-Levels flat where I grew up,
set in the bamboo grove - from the kumquat-
lined windows on the twenty-fifth floor,
tinted to bear the condensation's glare -
you can no longer see the insect cars
circling down those jungle-bordered boulevards.
The low-slung ferry, white above green,
piloting the harbour's carpet of stars,
turned always home, you can no longer see.

Islands

At the boarding school we used to chant them
Ping Chau, Cheung Chau, Lantau, Lamma …
I rolled their sounds around my mouth
till they were strange again, like savouring
those New Year candies - small translucent moons
waning on the tongue. Wrapped in packages
from home that never came. This was called
'geography', for knowing where we are and names
of fixed and distant things. The words came back to me
like dreams - sometimes only that insistent rhythm -
the rocking of the rope-prowed ferry, every minute
further from Macau, that isle of lotuses, my feet
slipping on the wet, wood deck, stretching up to feel
the terseness in the air, to catch the islands
swim like mist on the horizon. Passing fish huts perched
like spindly seabirds, foaming lacework
whispering into nothing on the rocks.
My heart was drowning - the long anticipated sight
of home. In the early years, we slept
three small girls to each shelf of the beds
like dumplings stacked in steamers, someone said.
Each night lifting the stout, sculpted planks
one at a time off the iron bedframe, knuckles tight.
Without a word, we let each end thud
heavy on the ground as though pounding
red beans into paste. The lice went running.
We squashed them with our sandaled feet but many
got away. We lay beneath that charcoal blanket
too heavy for the torpid summers; colour
of the August harbour in the rains.

We lay together breathing in that odour.
Sea-drizzle. Diesel. Damp, black hair.

    *

In October, typhoon season dwindles:
washed-out stars suspended in the puddles
where our faces floated by, white bellies of dead fish.
That year, before Mid-Autumn came we learned
to write 月. Haltingly, I penned the crescent
strokes of combinations from the board. It seemed
a ladder to the heavens, leading up and off
the yellowed page. The faded grid of squares grew
fainter. The desk beneath my hand was pocked
and battered like the surface of the moon. That
afternoon was following *Chang'e*. Her story.
One day, through curiosity, she swallowed down
a bright pill hidden in a box - *Houyi*'s Elixir of
Immortality. As he watched in horror, she floated
off into the thinning blue. Her long sleeves trailed
like cloud around a mountaintop, the moon
at first a pill, and then a swelling pearl, in the dark
mouth of the sky. He could not bear to shoot her
down with his star-felling bow. She lives there, cold
and lonely now. You can see her if you look.

    *

I often did. Waiting for the shadowed moon to rise
into the windowframe, a pale, dependable friend.
It took my mother many months to eat the gifts
of mooncakes; four cloud-encrusted islands drifting
in their silver tin. She would take a slice
each afternoon with cups of wine, the kind we
heated in a beaten kitchen pan. An autumn treat
accompanied by cooling evenings, too rich
for more habitual food. She cut into the patterned
casing. Full moon, half moon, quarter moon.
I loved the unexpected orb inside: a golden
yolk set in a firmament of lotus paste. They glowed
like all those tiny suns trapped in lanterns
at the festival, speared on slim red candles.
Their charring wicks were cedars twisted in the wind.
I had a paper globe. Its redness smouldered
like a burnt-out star. Other children had the shapes
of animals, crimson cellophane on wired frames -
the undulating waves of dragons, sharp-beaked
cranes, all in profile like the oval forms of fish.
In the blackness of Victoria Park their skin
was gleaming gelatine, the hatching chrysalides
of ghostly moths; a single, silver sequin
marked each winking, convex eye. The ruby
stain of lamplight over water. Fishlines trailed
from them, metallic ribbons - some fluttered off
like slanting rain to settle in the shrivelled grass.
The procession trod them in the moonlit dust.

*

The first thing I remember is the sickly
pungency of camphor. My mother hired me
a bedspace in the thin-partitioned tenement
we shared with other families, one of many.
It was summer. Sweltering in the box-space of her
plastered room, its single grime-barred window, heat
poured over us in humid troughs like the bilge
of a tropical sea. She lay on the floor, stiffly,
in the keel-shadow of the bed. I fanned her,
cross-legged, from the doorway. There was no other place.
The elastic in my underwear had gone. The swishing
fan was mouthing something in the dark; its silent arc
the wafting arms of underwater weeds. Her shiny face
was deep into the light-poured, drowning world
of sleep. I was four perhaps, or three. Small enough
to fit into the open wooden storage-chest
out in the hallway, freighted with that resinous
scent of aromatic lumber clinging to the moth-
proofed, folded winter clothes of the family
who held the let. It made a child-sized bed.
My dreams were diving through the fish-eye
glow of four electric candle-bulbs; their redness
hesitating on the finely spiralled filaments
the sidelights of a far-off ship. Or the microscopic
coal-flecks of the barely smoking joss sticks, sweet
to pacify the spirit tenants of their ancestral shrine.
The crinkled polaroids half-settled in the sand.
Their hungering voices; I slept inside my treasure chest.
Baby Moses flowing through the watermeadows.
She was always taking in abandoned things.
I think she saw her sadnesses reflected in them.
Once it was a stray puppy. She gave him to me.

But the next day, fawning, absently, gifted him
to strangers. Some years later, in her violent anger
I learned it was the same with me -
a Guangdong cobbler's foundling daughter. She
said she saved me from the refuse heap, from
being eaten by the dogs with other scraps.
Too many mouths to feed. I never wondered
about these unknown siblings. Or my father's
blackened hands, turning the warm hide
of a fraying shoe beneath his hammer.
Or my real mother. Unreachable across
the water, as planets circling in the night.

Mother's Jewellery Box

the twin lids
        of the black lacquer box
                open away -
a moonlit lake
        ghostly lotus leaves
                unfurl in tiers
silver chains
        careful *o*'s and *a*'s
                in copperplate

twisted strings
        of flattened beads
                lupin seeds

carnelians
        their tarnished settings
                horseflies' eyes

her amber ring -
        my fingers gauge
                its weight -

teaspoon of honey
        whisky poured
                by morning light

There is a Chinese proverb that says: 'It is more profitable to raise geese than daughters.' But geese, like daughters, know the obligation to return home. **Sarah Howe**, born in Hong Kong to an English father and Chinese mother, moved to England as a child. In her exquisite first collection, *Loop of Jade*, she explores a dual heritage, journeying back to Hong Kong in search of her roots.

 Emma-Lee Moss, who also grew up in Hong Kong, wrote in the *Guardian* that "I soon discovered that I couldn't read her book in public, for fear of crying in front of strangers... I know enough of the world she describes to be stunned by the accuracy with which she recovers certain experiences from the tide of history."

Loop of Jade is published by Chatto & Windus. The selections are reproduced by permission of The Random House Group Ltd.

David McKirdy

Outward Bound

Hannibal crossed The Alps
for conquest and glory.
We, adventurers of a different stripe
crossed the sea
destination Hong Kong
on the P&O liner
S.S. Carthage
built by fellow Scots, launched on our own River Clyde.

Up the gangway hand in hand we boarded
working class folk with boot-strap aspirations
to cabins
second class
the apartheid of imperial caste.
No P.O.S.H. travel for us but S.O.S.O. -
'Starboard out, staying out'
unlike that great general
never coming home
to disappointment and betrayal.

As we wave goodbye streamers sever our links
leaving monochrome memories and the 1950s in our wake
through Port Said, Suez, Aden and beyond
black-and-white Britain displaced, obscured
forgotten by senses now shaken by
shocking, pungent, grating
colours, odours and sounds
familiarity growing as we travel ever Eastward
warm and wet like a return to the womb.

Perhaps I'll linger here a while.

We Chinese

In Strasbourg, three Chinese asked for directions -

in French.

I answered -

in Cantonese.

Surprised -

they tried German.

Finally -

we expressed our pleasure
at meeting fellow countrymen abroad -

in English.

Star Struck

Star struck tourists
cliché their way across the harbour
in kitsch historic style
having scanned the brochures
and watched Nancy Kwan as Suzie Wong
sashay across the gangway.

But 50 years ago
Nancy Kwan as Nancy Kwan
travelled to and fro
there and back with the rest of us.
Downstairs for the unwashed masses
delivery bicycles with baskets of live chickens
British schoolboys
with long hair and a twenty-a-day habit
upstairs in first for the rest.

A burnished brass plaque declares:
'Hull built and machinery installed by
The Hong Kong and Whampoa Dock Company.'
My father built these vessels.
Northern Star, Night Star, Day Star
each one contains his essence
Shining Star, Twinkling Star
paid our school fees
Morning Star, Silver Star
put food on the table.

A Hong Kong icon
founded by Parsee merchants
designed by British shipwrights
built and crewed by Chinese working men.
The short trip between Island and Mainland
once a lifeline
now the tee-shirt experience
of a package tour
in our world city.

So government pragmatists moved the pier
surprised by a riot of protest -
the ghostly reminder
of bloodlines drawn in sand
the collective memory of a city divided
by race, ideology and fortune.

For years
governments have failed to listen.

It's our city
our heritage
our history.

Listen now.

A Red Guitar, Three Chords and the Truth

Jesus wants me for a sunbeam
or so I'm told
by guitar slingers on Sunday in the city
fanatical, evangelical, Filippinacal
with Fender Stratocasters and Marshall stacks.
Each group
more provocative than the next
louder than the Rolling Stones
but no sympathy for The Devil.
Jezebels with decibels
courting cash, canvassing for Christ.

In the cosseted comfort of the Mandarin Hotel
disgruntled guests get a rude awakening -

The call to prayer.

Bamboozled

The bamboo grove outside my bedroom clicks and clacks
a living breathing wind-chime
that whistles and whispers
the secrets of lives governed by seasons
unchanged for generations.

Hakka wanderers brought by the wind
came here
seduced to stay
by the sheltered cove
sweet fresh water
and these same soporific sounds.

I was the first foreigner for years
now we outnumber the villagers
and vote for each other at election time
neo-colonialists
seeking to civilise, educate
stop the building
stop the fishing
improve the marine ecology.

I voted for
Mr. Yeung Tin San
a Hakka elder
a realist who values tradition.
He was elected with a majority of one.

Sometimes I feel
the wind brought me here.

Working Class God

Across the nautical miles
on an island of fishermen
by the sheltered narrows of the China Sea
sits a house of God.
Built by the father's fathers of today's tillers of the waves
this temple is listed by the antiquities and monuments office
as a cultural icon of benefit to tourism
and scheduled for cleaning, re-tiling and restoration.
But it's listed as a part of life by these simple, honest folk
and scheduled for re-dedication and blessing.
For this is no Medici palace for an elegant effete and cultured deity
this is the home of a working class God with work to be done
controlling the elements, protecting the nets
and holding all vessels in a warm embrace.
Government bureaucrats, feathering their caps
want to preserve for posterity
the muted patinated tints and quaint dingy dank corners.
The villagers want a new brush to sweep clean
and paint in bright, lively, vibrant hues
of gaudily gold, red and green.
This house is not for a redundant God of antiquity
this God requires daily sustenance, libations and offerings.
He is part of the clan and everywhere visible;
in the sparkling of infinite pin pricks of light
as a gentle rain dapples the calm green sea
and deep amongst the ancient banyans
those sentinels with twisted limbs entwined in a sensual embrace
gnarled boughs that mirror the stooped backs of ancient mariners
themselves as hard and weathered as aged teak.

Now foreigners have come to Kau Sai Chau
Italians, offering their skills with open hands
that carry the genetic legacy
of Leonardo, Michelangelo, Botticelli, Caravaggio.
They delve with care amidst the treasures
and peel away the secrets of the years.
Uncovered scripts and ancient colours
reveal the hand of venerated generations
those long gone but ever present in nooks and crannies
in ancestral tablets and in the faces of boys at play.
The job is done, outsiders gone
life returns to the slow rhythmic pulse of the sea
and God rests his feet in front of the fire
at home with a cup of tea.

Shining

Mr. Lee the shoe-shine boy
is a proud man
still working at 82
still paying his way.
He'll shine my shoes for free
because I give him 'face'
calling him 'Uncle'
conversing, showing respect.

We're both immigrants
he from Indonesia
me from Scotland.
His generation made Hong Kong
today his clients read a paper
send a text
or gaze mutely at the top of his head.
He says I see into his heart
"Sir, what's your name?" he asks
"Chiu Chow Gum" I reply.
This is a euphemism for
crater-faced son of a bitch!
"That's a fine name" he says,
"No one will forget you."

I accept the gift of shiny shoes
and reciprocate with tea-money.
He claims to be the finest shiner in Hong Kong
he's certainly the best psychologist
I pay fifty bucks over the odds
and leave a happy man.

Homecoming

Flying home from the land of my birth
rituals performed, eulogy delivered
orphaned and pensive.
A little Chinese boy sleeps
with his head on my knee
trusting and innocent
I slide my pillow under him
and spread a blanket
as his mother snores beside him.
Later we chat
"Uncle, are you a foreigner?"
"Yes, born in Scotland."
"Why can you speak Cantonese?"
"I am a Hong Kong man now."
"How old are you?"
"55, and you?"
"I am 5 years old."
Just a year older than me
when I left
traveling towards a new life.
50 years absence has made me
a venerable uncle
with an inscrutable Western smile
heading back to my Chinese home.

Senior Citizen

I've been to some funerals lately;
a teacher or two
friends and relatives.
My mother, my father.

They smile and thumb their noses
as they pass on the burden
and quietly slip off to another place
of timeless tenure.

We consulted our elders and betters
now, I'm an elder and better
for better or worse
but no consultations so far.

What will I say, what will I do
will wisdom emerge,
or elude me?

As my time rushes on
like the wind from the North.

Epistle to my unborn child

You missed your chance at life
because I jealously nurtured mine.
Because of commitment;
Absolute when it came to personal goals
absolutely lacking when it came to relationships
and letting go of fear and the baggage of insecurity.

I never gave myself permission to love or be loved.
The possibility of you frightened me in early years.
You were absent as a concept as I pursued fame and fortune
and the motorcycle world championship.
You merited not a thought as I traversed the world
entranced by the glamour of Formula One.

I matured reluctantly into a middle-aged teenager
and sought acclaim as a rock musician.
Your voice was seldom heard
just an occasional appearance in thoughts and dreams
and the nagging doubt
that time was passing by.

But now, as I more often put my thoughts on paper
you appear daily and appeal to me.
So many of my friends are fathers, mothers, grandfathers!
I'm twice a Godfather, but never the real thing.
Did I miss a chance, or did they?
Or have we missed it yet?

David McKirdy is one of Hong Kong's best-known poets. He was born in Scotland, raised in Hong Kong and confused in England when he arrived there for the first time as a twenty-year-old. Once he returned to Hong Kong, he never left again.

Unlike many poets, he came to writing relatively late in life, after a varied career that included a stint as a professional musician and racing motorcycles on the Hong Kong international team. He remains one of Hong Kong's leading experts on the workings of classic and antique cars.

His poetry deals with the Hong Kong of his youth and his relationship with the modern-day city that he has grown up with. Some of the pieces tackle the relationship between the colonisers and the colonised in British Hong Kong during the 1960s and 70s, when it was still a colony with a capital C and inequality and unfairness was rife. Other poems tackle how attitudes and approaches changed from the late 1960s onwards, coinciding with his own teenage years and political and social awakening.

The poems here are taken from his two collections *Ancestral Worship* and *Accidental Occidental*, published by Chameleon Press.